PRJC
2/17

Puffer Fish

by Joyce Markovics

Consultant: Thane Maynard, Director
Cincinnati Zoo and Botanical Garden
Cincinnati, Ohio

BEARPORT
PUBLISHING

New York, New York

Credits

Cover, © Andrey Nekrasov/Alamy; TOC, © Dariush M/Shutterstock; 5, © Tsuneo Nakamura/Volvox Inc/Alamy; 7, © Flame/Alamy; 8, © Johannes Kornelius/Shutterstock; 9, © serg_dibrova/Shutterstock; 10T, © LauraD/Shutterstock; 10M, © Mathee Suwannarak/Shutterstock; 10B, © Dray van Beeck/Shutterstock; 10–11, © age fotostock/Alamy; 12, © SeaPics.com; 12–13, © Cigdem Sean Cooper/Shutterstock; 14–15, © mokee81/iStock; 16, © ligio/Shutterstock; 17, © Moize nicolas/Shutterstock; 18–19, © elzeva/iStock; 20–21, © Dariush M/Shutterstock; 22T, © Chris Hill/Shutterstock; 22M, © creativex/Shutterstock; 22B, © Mogens Trolle/Shutterstock; 23TL, © leungchopan/Shutterstock; 23TR, © Andrea Izzotti/Shutterstock; 23BL, © urbancow/iStock; 23BR, © Napat_Polchoke/iStock.

Publisher: Kenn Goin
Senior Editor: Joyce Tavolacci
Creative Director: Spencer Brinker
Design: Debrah Kaiser
Photo Researcher: Olympia Shannon

Library of Congress Cataloging-in-Publication Data

Markovics, Joyce L., author.
  Puffer fish / by Joyce Markovics.
      pages cm. — (Weird but cute)
  Summary: "In this book, readers will meet the cute but weird puffer fish"— Provided by publisher.
  Audience: Ages 5–8.
  Includes bibliographical references and index.
  ISBN 978-1-62724-850-1 (library binding) — ISBN 1-62724-850-1 (library binding)
  1. Puffers (Fish)—Juvenile literature. I. Title.
  QL638.T32M37 2016
  597'.64—dc23
                              2015007541

For more information, write to Bearport Publishing Company, Inc., 45 West 21st Street, Suite 3B, New York, New York 10010. Printed in the United States of America.

10 9 8 7 6 5 4 3 2 1

Contents

What's this weird
but cute animal?

It's a
puffer fish.

Big **eye**s!

R**O**und,
spiky body!
5

Some puffers are very tiny.

Others are as big as basketballs.

There are more than 120 kinds of puffer fish.

giant puffer

Unlike most fish, puffers do not have **scales**.

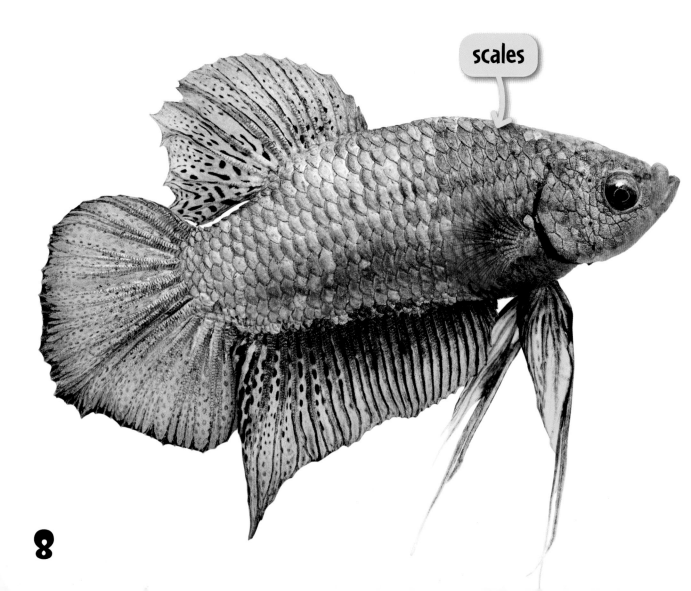

scales

They have smooth skin.

smooth skin

Some puffers have small spikes on their skin.

Each kind of puffer has a different skin **pattern**.

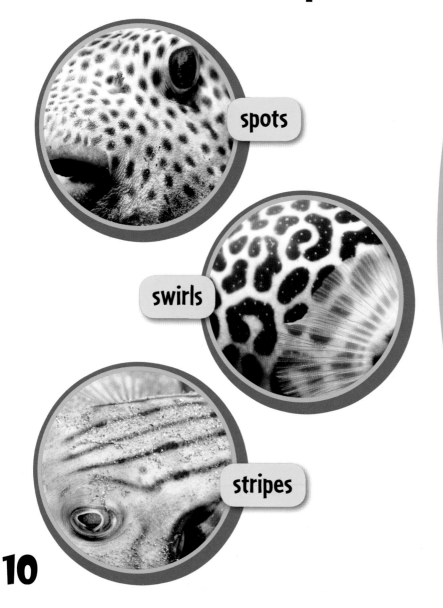

spots

swirls

stripes

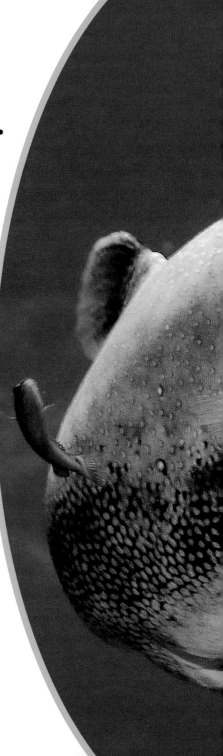

These fish come in many colors.

Puffers can change their skin color!

Is that a bird's **beak**?

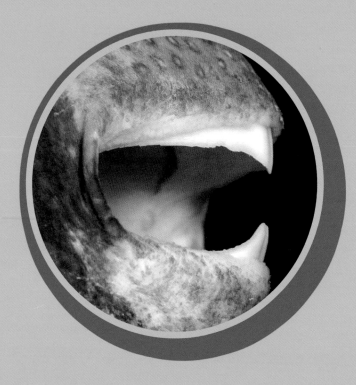

No, it's a puffer fish's four large teeth.

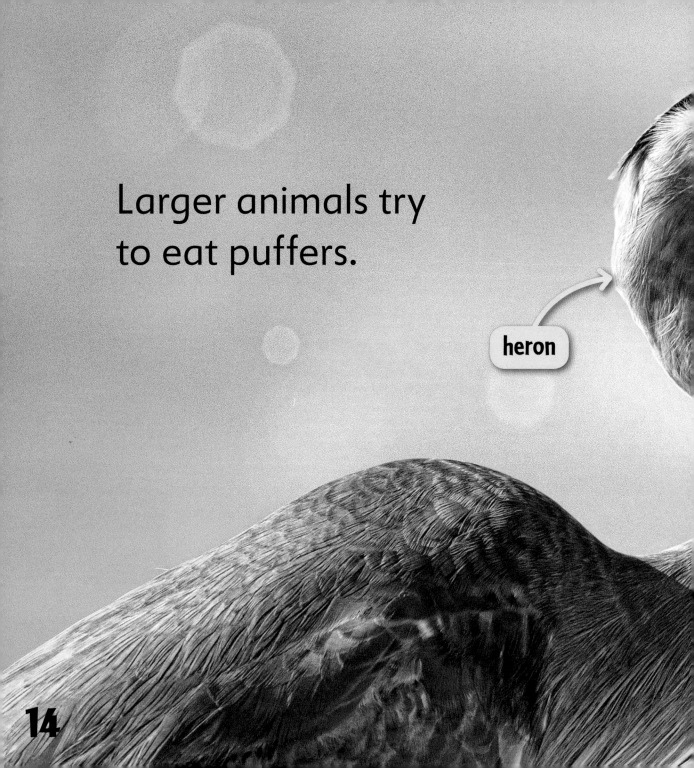

Larger animals try to eat puffers.

heron

That's when
puffer fish puff up!

15

Gulp. Gulp. Gulp. Puffers swallow lots of water or air.

Their bodies blow up like balloons.

To enemies, they look too big to eat!

a puffer before blowing up

Puffer fish are also known as blowfish.

a puffer after blowing up

Puffers stay safe in another way.

Did you know that their bodies contain **poison**?

The poison in one puffer can kill 30 people!

Puffer poison is one of the deadliest poisons in the world.

Puffers can swim up,
down, forward, and
backward.

They can zip through
the water—*zoom!*

Look quickly before they're gone.

fin

Puffer fish use
their fins to move
through the water.

More Puffy Animals

American Bullfrog
The American bullfrog has a big sac under its throat. When the frog croaks, the sac looks like a giant bubble.

Elephant Seal
Male elephant seals have huge, puffy noses that can be 1 foot (30.5 cm) long. The seals fill their noses with air and snort loudly to scare off other males.

Frigate Bird
The frigate bird is a large seabird. The male has a puffy red pouch on its throat that it uses to attract females. When filled with air, the pouch is almost half the size of the bird!

Glossary

beak (BEEK) a hard, pointy mouthpart used for eating

pattern (PAT-urn) a set of markings, such as stripes or spots

poison (POI-zuhn) something that can kill or harm a living thing

scales (SKAYLZ) small pieces of hard skin that cover the bodies of most fish

Index

Read More

Rake, Jody Sullivan. *Puffer Fish (Under the Sea).* North Mankato, MN: Capstone (2007).

Sexton, Colleen. *Puffer Fish (Oceans Alive).* Minneapolis, MN: Bellwether Media (2008).

Learn More Online

To learn more about puffer fish, visit
www.bearportpublishing.com/WeirdButCute

About the Author

Joyce Markovics is a writer and editor who lives along the Hudson River in New York. She has two pet puffer fish, which rarely get puffy.